Sally

Lehrwerk für den
Englischunterricht ab Klasse 3

Activity Book 4
Förderheft

Erarbeitet von
Martina Bredenbröcker
Jasmin Brune
Daniela Elsner
Barbara Gleich
Stefanie Gleixner-Weyrauch
Simone Gutwerk
Martina Koch
Marion Lugauer
Sabine Schwarz

Unter Beratung von Jane Brockmann-Fairchild

Portfolio: Nina Winnertz

Illustriert von Barbara Jung, Wilfried Poll,
Thilo Pustlauk, Gisela Vogel

 Deine interaktiven Gratis-Übungen findest du hier:

1. Gehe auf scook.de.
2. Gib den unten stehenden Zugangscode in die Box ein.
3. Hab viel Spaß mit deinen Gratis-Übungen.

Dein Zugangscode auf
www.scook.de

Die Gratis-Übungen können dort
nach Bestätigung der AGB und
Lizenzbedingungen genutzt werden.

byowx-cmeh4

Oldenbourg Schulbuchverlag, München

Inhalt

Special days:

Sally 4 Activity Book Förderheft © 2015 Cornelsen Schulverlage GmbH, Berlin

Numbers

1 ✂️✏️ **Cut out the puzzle (page 43), match the numbers and stick in.**

two	four	nine	seven
six	eight	three	five
eleven	ten	twelve	one

2 ✏️ **Match the numbers to the words.**

twenty
ten
one hundred
fifty
forty

10 70 50 60 100 40 20 80 30 90

seventy
eighty
ninety
sixty
thirty

⭐ **Count backwards from 20 to 1.**

Sally 4 Activity Book Förderheft © 2015 Cornelsen Schulverlage GmbH, Berlin

What time is it?

1 🔘 ✏️ **Listen and number the clocks.**

☐ [clock showing ~8:45] ☐ [clock showing ~6:30] 1 [clock showing ~3:20] 3 [clock showing ~11:00] ☐ [clock showing ~6:00]

2 🔘 ✏️ **Listen and tick ✔ the correct time.**

37 +48=

What time is it?

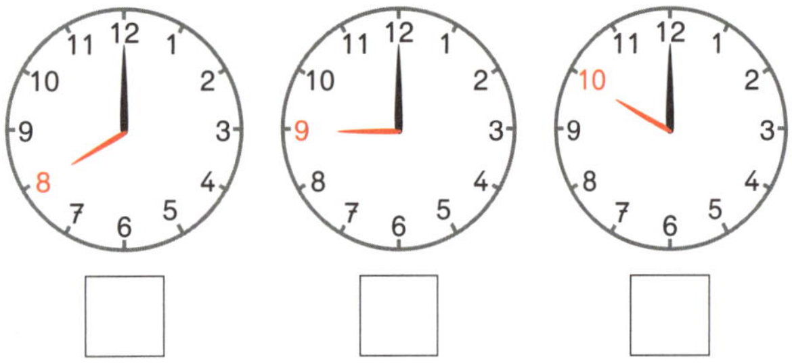

[clock ~8:35] [clock ~9:00] [clock ~10:15]

☐   ☐   ☐

What do frogs eat?

What time is it now?

[clock ~10:00] [clock ~11:05] [clock ~12:00]

☐   ☐   ☐

Robin Hood

What time is it?

[clock ~11:05] [clock ~12:00] [clock ~12:30]

☐   ☐   ☐

I'm so hungry!

Lunchtime!

Sally 4 Activity Book Förderheft © 2015 Cornelsen Schulverlage GmbH, Berlin

The time

1  **Draw lines.**

It's half past two.   It's half past twelve.   It's nine o'clock.

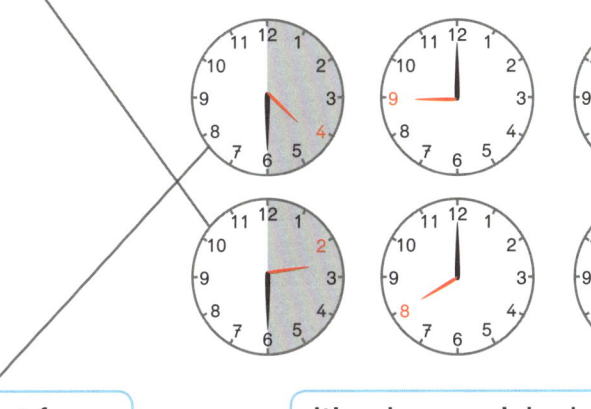

It's half past four.   It's eleven o'clock.   It's eight o'clock.

2 Set the clock. Draw the clock's hands.

  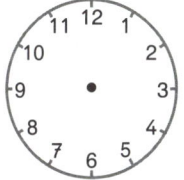 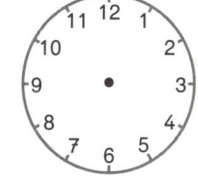

It's one o'clock.   It's half past six.   It's four o'clock.   It's half past seven.

3 What time is it? Write.

 It's   two o'clock.

 _____ twelve _____ .

 It's half past four.

 It's half past eight.

 It's ten o'clock.

 _____ seven .

4 Fill in your portfolio.

Sally 4 Activity Book Förderheft © 2015 Cornelsen Schulverlage GmbH, Berlin

Rooms

1 ✏️ **Write the names of the rooms.**

1 bedroom   2 bedroom   3 bathroom

4 toilet   5 kitchen   6 living room

2 ✏️ **Where are they? Write.**

kitchen
bathroom
bedroom
toilet
living room

 Where is Father Ghost? He is in the bedroom .

 Where is Mother Ghost? She is in the _ _ _ _ _ _ _ _ _.

 Where is Sister Ghost? She is in the _ _ _ _ _ _ _ _.

 Where is Gavin? He is in the _ _ _ _ _ _ _ _ _ _ _.

 Where is the mouse? It is in the _ _ _ _ _ _ _.

 Where is the cat? It is in the _ _ _ _ _ _ _ _ _.

Salty 4 Activity Book Förderheft © 2015 Cornelsen Schulverlage GmbH, Berlin

Too big, too small or just right?

1 ✏️✂️ **Is it just right? Read, choose your answer, write and draw.**

| Yes, it's just right. | No, it's too big. | No, it's too small. |

Is the **bath** just right for Sally?

No, it's too small.

Is the **sofa** just right for Sally?

● No, it's too big.

Is the **wardrobe** just right for Sally?

Yes, it's just right.

Is the **chair** just right for Sally?

_____ .

●

Is the **bed** just right for Sally?

_____ .

Is the **table** just right for Sally?

_____ .

2 ✏️ **Fill in your portfolio.**

Let's make a sandwich!

1 ✏️ **Find the words and circle ⬭ them.**

lettuce ketchup
ham cucumber
bread cheese
tomato mustard

t y l e t t u c e l k h a m
j a c u c u m b e r f e r u
o l m k t z u c h e e s e p
u t o m a t o e n b r e a d
p o l m u s t a r d u t r k
p o q u y k e t c h u p a b

2 ✏️✏️ **Draw your own sandwich. Write down what you put on it.**

_____

_____

_____

_____

3 💿 **Read and sing.**

The sandwich rap

1. I am hungry, can't you see?
   I'll make a sandwich, listen to me.
   Yum, yum the sandwich rap.

2. All I have, I put on it.
   This sandwich makes me really fit.
   Yum, yum the sandwich rap.

3. Bread, tomatoes and some cheese,
   and I need some ketchup, please.
   Yum, yum the sandwich rap.

4. Ketchup, ham and bread on top –
   now I really have to stop.
   Yum, yum the sandwich rap.

5. It's so big, it's so big, it's a big, big one!
   Too bad, too bad, soon it's all gone!
   Oh!
   Yum, yum the sandwich rap.

Sally 4 Activity Book Förderheft © 2015 Cornelsen Schulverlage GmbH, Berlin

It's time for lunch!

1 **Read the menu and colour the trays.**

MENU **Monday**
1. tomato soup
2. salad with cheese

MENU **Tuesday**
1. sausage with mashed potatoes
2. carrot soup

MENU **Wednesday**
1. fish and chips
2. ham sandwich

MENU **Thursday**
1. spaghetti
2. cheese sandwich

MENU **Friday**
1. salad with ham
2. pizza

2  **Write your own menu plan. Tell your partner.**

Monday: _____

Tuesday: _____

Wednesday: _____

Thursday: _____

Friday: _____

_____

⭐ **Choose a drink for your menu plan.**

Sally 4 Activity Book Förderheft © 2015 Cornelsen Schulverlage GmbH, Berlin

Let's have lunch

Let's lay the table!

1 ✎ **Lay the table for eight people and draw.**

2 ✎ **What was missing? Write.**

4 forks, __ plates, 3 knives, __ cup, __ spoon, __ glasses

3 ✎ **Which answer is correct? Write. Cross out the wrong picture.**

You pick up food with it: It's a fork .

 You eat soup with it: It's a _ _ _ _ _ _ .

You need it for cutting: It's a _ _ _ _ _ _ .

You put lemonade in it: It's a _ _ _ _ _ _ .

You eat from it: It's a _ _ _ _ _ .

 You drink tea out of it: It's a _ _ _ _ .

fork plate knife cup spoon glass

Sally 4 Activity Book Förderheft © 2015 Cornelsen Schulverlage GmbH, Berlin

In the restaurant

1 **Listen and circle ◯ the correct picture.**

 Can I help you?

 I'd like a , please.

 Would you like something to drink?

 Yes, I'd like a glass of   , please.

 That's £1 (£2) £4 , please.

 Two pounds. Here you are.

 Can I help you?

 I'd like a   , please.

 Anything to drink?

 Yes, I'd like a glass of   , please.

 That's £1.50 £3.20 (£2.30) , please.

 Two pounds 30. Here you are.

2  **Read the menu. Make up the dialogue.**

3 **Say the tongue twister.**

Sly Sam slurps Sally's soup.

4 **Fill in your portfolio.**

FOOD

pizza £1
hamburger £1
salad with ham £1.20
tomato soup £1
cheese sandwich £1
chicken sandwich £1.30

DRINKS

orange juice £1
coke £1
lemonade £1
tea £1
coffee £1
water £1

Sally 4 Activity Book Förderheft © 2015 Cornelsen Schulverlage GmbH, Berlin

What's your hobby?

1 **Draw lines.**

swimming

riding a bike

playing the guitar

reading books

ice skating

playing the piano

snowboarding

playing football

riding a horse

2 **Complete the sentences.**

 Susan likes riding a horse.

 Tim likes riding a bike

and _____ .

 Emily likes ice skating

and _____ .

 Eric likes _____ .

 Phil likes snowboarding

and _____ .

 Liz _____ .

Sally 4 Activity Book Förderheft © 2015 Cornelsen Schulverlage GmbH, Berlin

This is me!

1 💿✏️ **Listen. Write the missing words.**

My name is _____ .

I'm _____ years old.

I live in London .

My hobby is reading books

and _____ .

I'm in class 4f .

My favourite food is _____ .

I like _____ .

London ~~London~~   pizza   ~~reading books~~

ten   ~~4f~~   Phil   snowboarding   dogs

2 ✏️✂️✏️ **Write about yourself.**
Draw a picture of yourself or stick in a photo.
Read your text to your class.

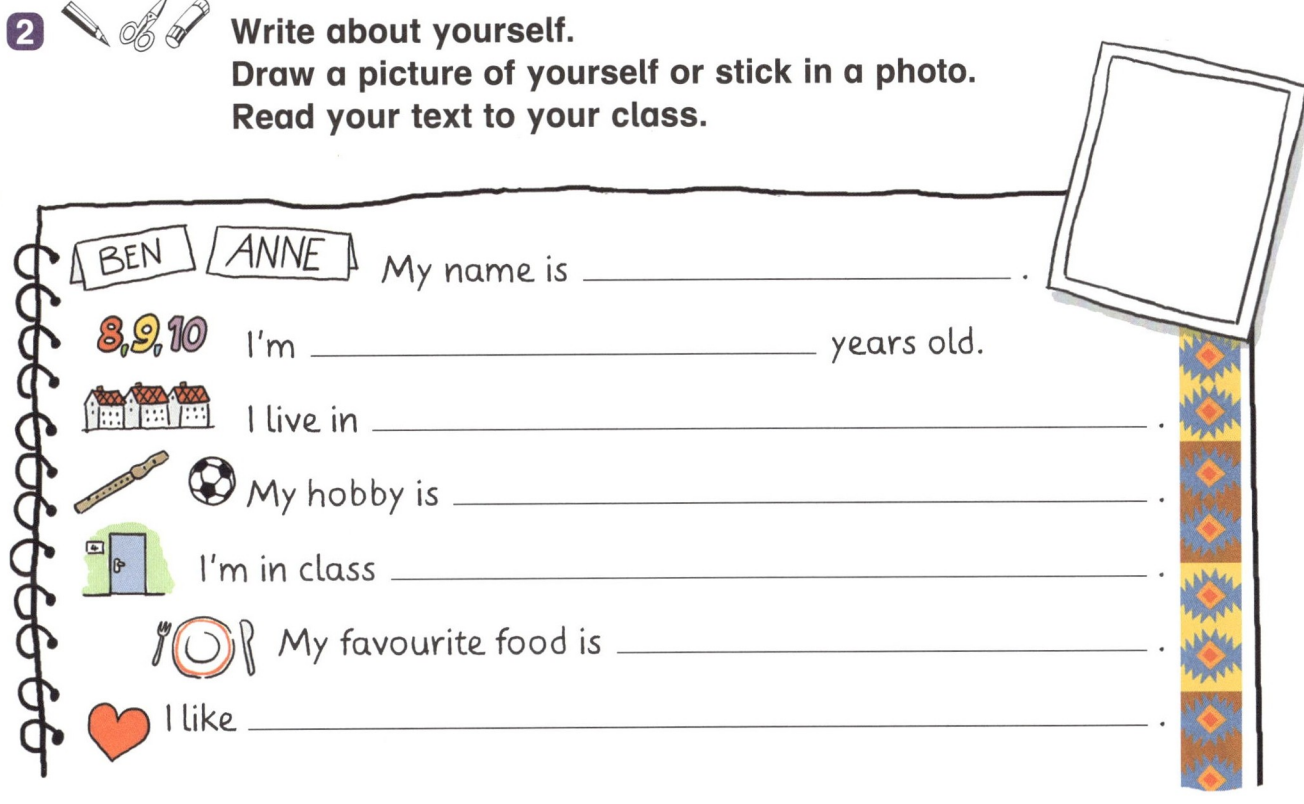

BEN ANNE My name is _____ .

8, 9, 10 I'm _____ years old.

I live in _____ .

My hobby is _____ .

I'm in class _____ .

My favourite food is _____ .

♥ I like _____ .

An interview with a sports star

1  **Read, listen and number. Write.**

	Thank you for the interview.	4	Yes, I can.
6	No, I can't.	2	Hi, I'm fine, thanks.
	Hi, Dirk. How are you?		Can you play golf?
	Can you play football?		

Hi, I'm fine, thanks.

Yes, I can.

No, I can't.

2  **Read the interview. Work with a partner.**

Sally 4 Activity Book Förderheft © 2015 Cornelsen Schulverlage GmbH, Berlin

The sporty rap

1 Listen to the rap.

2 Write the missing words.

The sporty rap

I do it. It's okay .

I like it when I _____ .

I do it. It's fun .

● I like it when I _____ .

I do it. It's great .

I like it when I _____ .

Playing, running, skating, riding after _____ ?

Yes, we _____ it!

Yes, we _____ it!

Yes, we do !

| skate | ~~fun~~ | ~~okay~~ | run | ~~great~~ |
| play | school | ~~do~~ | love | like |

● **3** Read the skipping rhymes.

Apples, peaches, pears and plums,
tell me when your birthday comes.
January, February, March …

I like coffee, I like tea,
I want Sally to jump with me.
One, two, three …

Teddy bear, teddy bear, turn around.

Teddy bear, teddy bear, touch the ground.

Teddy bear, teddy bear, show your shoe.

Teddy bear, teddy bear, that will do!

Teddy bear, teddy bear, go upstairs.

Teddy bear, teddy bear, say your prayers.

Teddy bear, teddy bear, turn out the light.

Teddy bear, teddy bear, say good night!

4 Fill in your portfolio.

Sally 4 Activity Book Förderheft © 2015 Cornelsen Schulverlage GmbH, Berlin

My day

Through the day

1 🔘 **Listen to the song.**

2 ✂️✏️ **Cut out the text (page 43), match and stick it in.**

3 ✏️ **Set the clock. Draw the clock's hands.**

Hickory, dickory, dock!
The mouse ran up the clock.
The clock struck one.
The mouse ran down.
Hickory, dickory, dock!

At eight o'clock in the morning ...

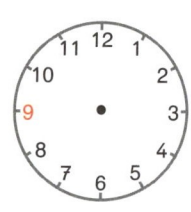 

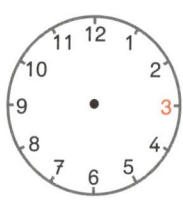 

At eight o'clock in the evening ...

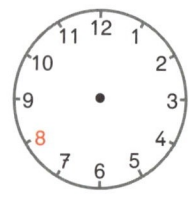 

Sally 4 Activity Book Förderheft © 2015 Cornelsen Schulverlage GmbH, Berlin

One day in the life of Alpha 72

1 Listen.

2 Cut out the pictures (page 45), match and stick them in.

3 Write the missing words.

At 3 o'clock

I _____ .

At half past 3 I have

_____ .

At quarter to 4

I _____ my hair.

At 6 o'clock I
go to school .
We learn to fly.

At quarter past 10
I have lunch .

At 1 o'clock
I do my homework .

At 2 o'clock

I _____ with my pet.

At half past 4

I _____ my friends.

At 6 o'clock

I _____ .

4 Fill in your portfolio.

learn   go to bed   get up   brush   ~~go to school~~
breakfast   call   lunch   ~~do my homework~~   play

Sally 4 Activity Book Förderheft © 2015 Cornelsen Schulverlage GmbH, Berlin

In the supermarket

1 ✎ **Read and write.**

| orange juice bread eggs milk honey cheese spinach oranges |
| ice cream biscuits chocolate bars apples lemonade ham |

milk

biscuits honey

lemonade orange juice

Phil's shopping list:

eggs

lemonade

spinach

chocolate bars

milk

cheese

spinach ice cream

2  **Listen and circle** ◯ . **3** ✎ **Write Phil's shopping list.**

Sally 4 Activity Book Förderheft © 2015 Cornelsen Schulverlage GmbH, Berlin

PARKING (11)   (12) TOILETS

WOMEN   MEN

TOYS PARADISE (7)

BEST CLOTHES 4 YOU (8)

Music&More (3)

SUPER SPORTS (4)

2 ✎ **Where can the children buy these things? Read and write.**

> Excuse me, please. Where can I buy a book?

Go to Mickey's Books.
It's on the ground floor.

> Excuse me, please. Where can I buy a pair of boots?

Go to Perfect Shoes.
It's on the _____ floor.

> Excuse me, please. Where can I buy a new computer game?

Go to Computer & Games World.
It's on the _____.

> Excuse me, please. Where can I buy a lollipop?

Go to Sweets.
_____.

3 🐾 **You are at the shopping centre. Ask your way.**

Sally 4 Activity Book Förderheft © 2015 Cornelsen Schulverlage GmbH, Berlin

In the shop

1 🔘 ✏️ **Listen and tick ✔ the correct answer.**

Jacket number 1	Jacket number 2	Liz buys
☐ is too small.	☐ is black.	☐ a big jacket.
☐ is too big.	☐ is blue.	☐ a brown jacket.
☐ is just right.	☐ is brown.	✔ a stylish jacket.

Liz pays	Phil must go
☐ £5.	☐ to school.
☐ £20.	☐ to the toilet.
✔ £25.	☐ to the toy shop.

2 🔘 ✂️ ✏️ **Listen. Cut out the speech bubbles 💬 (page 43), match and stick them in.**

Hello. Can I help you?

How about this one? Try it on.

It's £25.

Thank you. Goodbye.

3 ✏️ **Fill in your portfolio.**

Sally 4 Activity Book Förderheft © 2015 Cornelsen Schulverlage GmbH, Berlin

Jack and the beanstalk

1 🔘 **Listen to the story.**

2 ✂️ **Cut out the pictures (page 47).**

3 ✏️ **Match and stick them in.**

> Fee, fi, foe, fum!
> I smell the blood of
> an Englishman.

⭐ **What fairy tales do you know? Show your books in class.**

4 ✏️ **Fill in your portfolio.**

Sally 4 Activity Book Förderheft © 2015 Cornelsen Schulverlage GmbH, Berlin

Flying to London

1 ✎ **Fill in your boarding pass to London.**

AIRLINE: England Airline

NAME: _____

NAME: _____

FLIGHT NUMBER: **FLIGHT:**   **DATE:**

EA 21   _____   _____

GATE: BOARDING TIME: SEAT NUMBER:

B1   10 o'clock   A 4

2 ✎ **Read the sentences. What's wrong? Cross out the wrong words. Write the correct sentences.**

In London the taxis are ~~green~~/black.

     In London the taxis are _____ .

You can take the ferry/underground on the River Thames.

     You can take the _____ on the River Thames .

The red double-decker car/bus is very famous.

     The red double-decker _____ is very famous .

In London cars and buses drive on the left-hand/right-hand side of the road.

     In London cars and buses drive on the _____-_____ side

of the road .

Sally 4 Activity Book Förderheft © 2015 Cornelsen Schulverlage GmbH, Berlin

Detective Brighthead

1 💿 **Listen and number the vehicles.**

2 💿 ✏️ **Listen again. Where do they go?**
Draw lines.

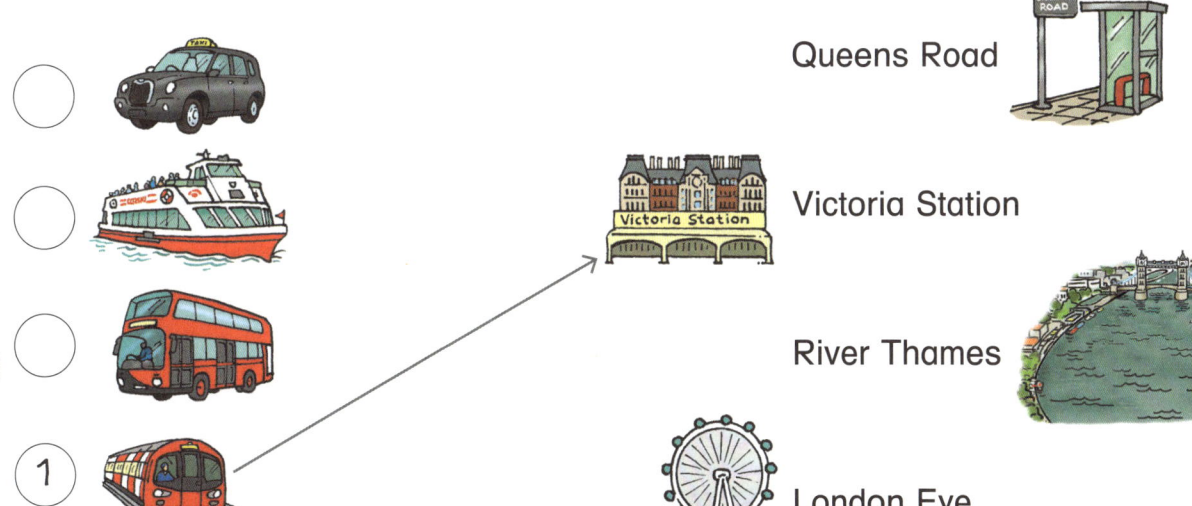

Queens Road

Victoria Station

River Thames

London Eye

3 ✏️ **Read and draw lines.**

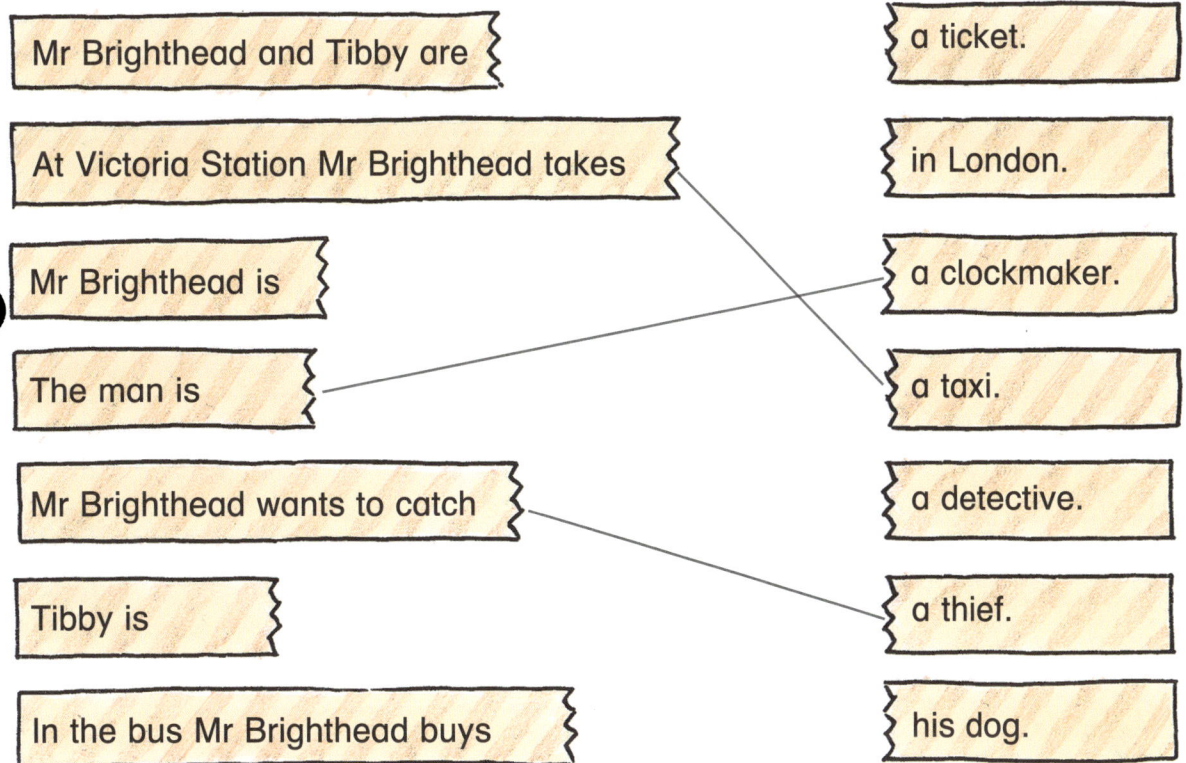

Mr Brighthead and Tibby are	a ticket.
At Victoria Station Mr Brighthead takes	in London.
Mr Brighthead is	a clockmaker.
The man is	a taxi.
Mr Brighthead wants to catch	a detective.
Tibby is	a thief.
In the bus Mr Brighthead buys	his dog.

⭐ **Write down the sentences in the correct order.**

Map of London

1 💬 **Which vehicles can you take?**
At the London Eye I can take the ferry. At Big Ben …

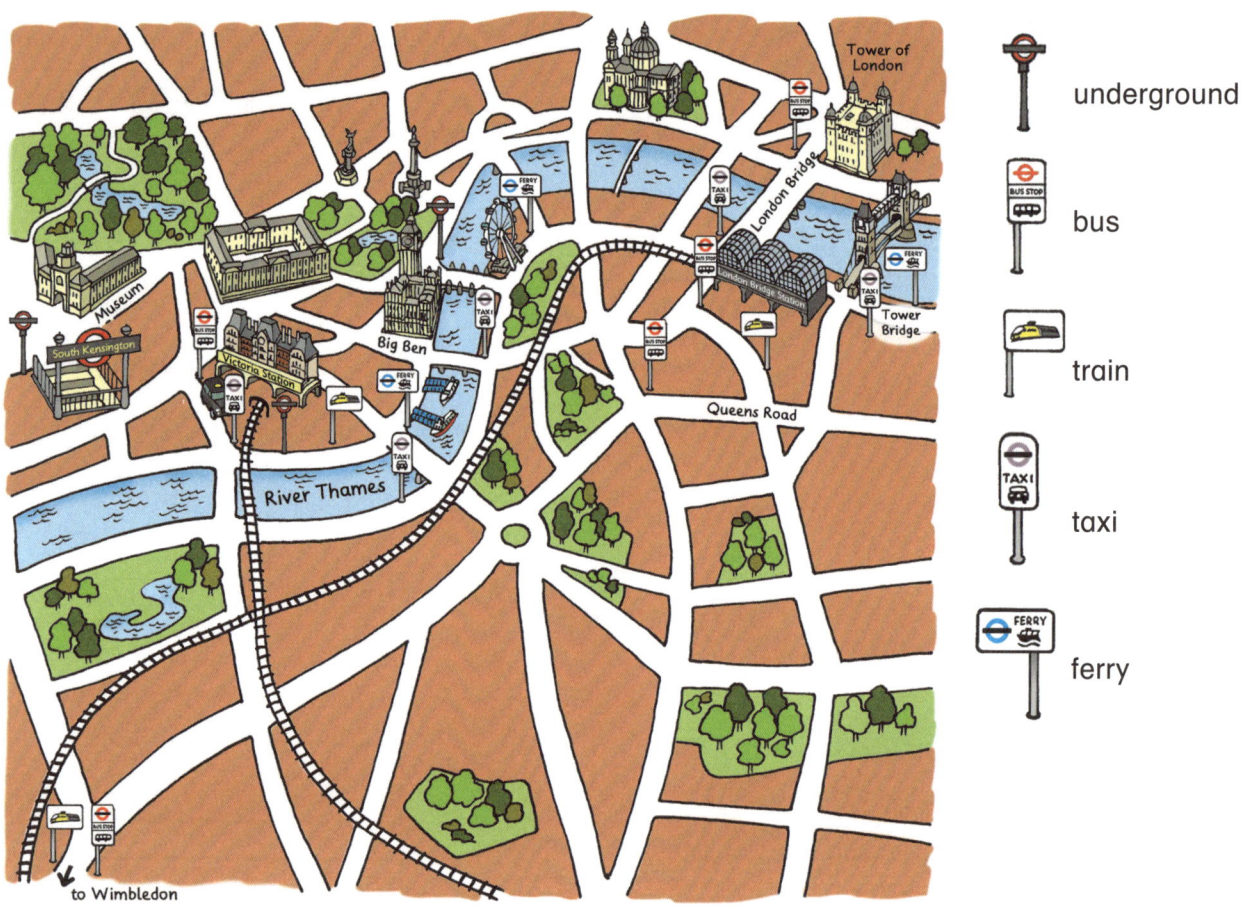

2 💿✏️ **Listen and complete the sentences.**

How can I go from London Bridge to Wimbledon?

You can take the **train** or the _____.

How can I go from Big Ben to Tower Bridge?

You can take the **ferry** or a _____.

3 🐾 **Ask your partner for the way.**

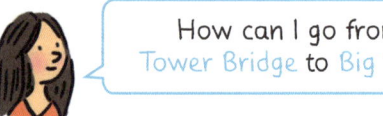

How can I go from Tower Bridge to Big Ben?

You can take the ferry or a taxi.

4 ✏️ **Fill in your portfolio.**

Animals of the wild

1 🖊 **Read and draw lines. Write and tell.**

giraffe

tortoise

lion

zebra

hippo

● elephant

monkey

fast

clever

tall

funny

fat

dangerous

big

2 🖊 **Do the crossword.**

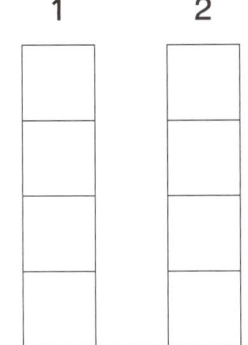

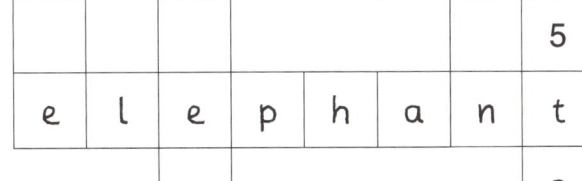
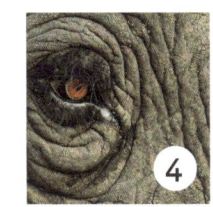

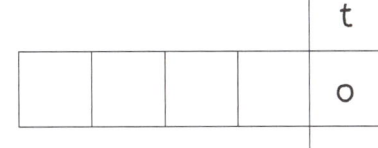

4 across: e l e p h a n t

5 down: t o r t o i s e

snake giraffe lion zebra monkey
elephant hippo tortoise

Sally 4 Activity Book Förderheft © 2015 Cornelsen Schulverlage GmbH, Berlin

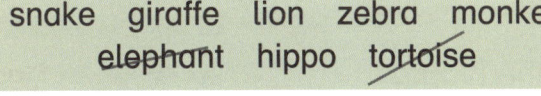

 **Wild animals**

Walking through the jungle

1 🎵 ✏️ **Listen to the song. Write in the missing words.**

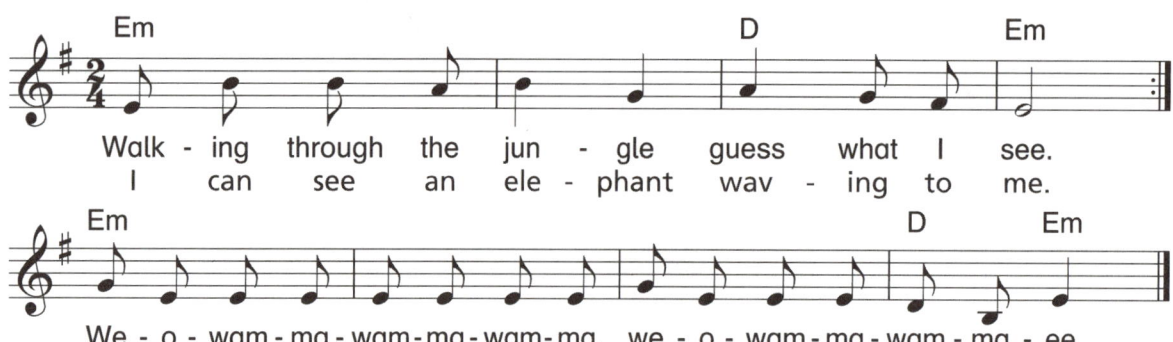

Em   D   Em

Walk - ing   through   the   jun - gle   guess   what   I   see.
I   can   see   an   ele - phant   wav - ing   to   me.

Em   D   Em

We - o - wam - ma - wam - ma - wam - ma,   we - o - wam - ma - wam - ma - ee

1. Walking through the 🌴 jungle , guess what I see?

   I can see an 🐘 _ _ _ _ _ _ _ _ _ _ _ waving to me.

2. I can see a tall 🦒 _ _ _ _ _ _ _ _ looking down at me.

3. I can see a 🦛 _ _ _ _ _ _ yawning ooh – aah – eeh.

4. I can see a 🦓 _ _ _ _ _ running fast to me.

5. I can see a 🐒 _ _ _ _ _ _ climbing in a tree.

Can you go on?   I can see _____ .

> elephant   monkey   jungle   zebra   giraffe   hippo

The clever tortoise

2 🎵 ✏️ **Listen and tick ✔: yes or no**

	yes	no
The tortoise, the monkey and the snake live in Africa.	☐	☐
One day there is a big party.	☐	✔
The zebra is the king of the jungle.	☐	☐
The clever tortoise has got an idea.	☐	☐
The hippo and the elephant play tennis.	☐	☐
The tortoise plays a trick on the elephant and the hippo.	✔	☐

Sally 4 Activity Book Förderheft © 2015 Cornelsen Schulverlage GmbH, Berlin

My animal

1  **Look at your animal. Write a riddle and read it to your classmates.**

It has got …
… legs
… arms
… a trunk
… wings
… a tail

It's …
… small, big, tall, long
… fat, strong, fast
… funny, clever, dangerous
… brown, white, grey, green

It can …
… climb
… swim
… jump
… run
… fly
… bite

It lives …
… in the jungle
… in the zoo
… in the sea
… in the forest
… in trees

My animal has got _____

It's _____

It can _____

It lives _____

_____

2 ✏ **Fill in your portfolio.**

Sally 4 Activity Book Förderheft © 2015 Cornelsen Schulverlage GmbH, Berlin

At the doctor's

1 ✏ **Number and write the words.**

1 headache   2 earache

3 neckache   4 backache

2 ✏ **Complete the sentences.**

I'm sick.

My [ear] hurts.

I've got an [earache] .

I'm sick.

My _____ [hurts] .

I've got a _____ .

I'm [sick] .

My _____ _____ .

I've got a _____ .

I'm _____

My _____

I've got a _____

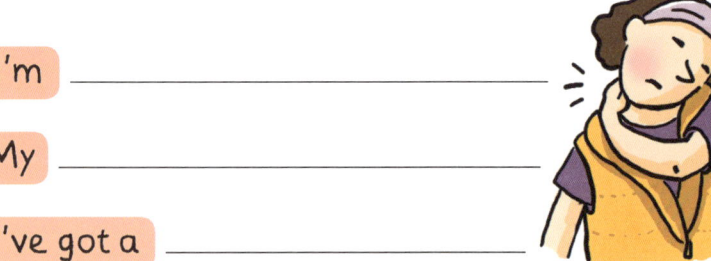

I've got **an e**arache.

I've got **a b**ackache.

neck ~~ear~~ back head headache
backache ~~earache~~ neckache

Sally 4 Activity Book Förderheft © 2015 Cornelsen Schulverlage GmbH, Berlin

The inline skating accident

1  **Listen. Cut out the speech bubbles ⃝ (page 45). Match and stick them in.**

What's the matter?

Your hand is not broken. Let's put some ice on it.

2 **Act out the story.**

3 ✏ **Fill in your portfolio.**

Sally 4 Activity Book Förderheft © 2015 Cornelsen Schulverlage GmbH, Berlin

Sally and the Loch Ness Monster

1 🎧 **Listen to the story. Read and tick ✔ the correct words.**

My uncle Tom ✔
My uncle Tim ☐   lives in Scotland.
My aunt Tom ☐

Welcome to Scotland!

Welcome to Scotland! ☐
England! ☐
Germany! ☐

The next morning the kangaroos go to   Lake Ness. ☐
Loch Ness. ☐
Look Ness. ☐

The next day they are sleeping ☐
sitting ✔   at the breakfast table.
standing ☐

Back home, the kangaroos look at the souvenirs ☐
books ☐   of their trip.
photos ☐

Sally 4 Activity Book Förderheft © 2015 Cornelsen Schulverlage GmbH, Berlin

A trip to Scotland

1 ✏️ **Fill in the missing words.**

l _____

r _____

c _____

s ____

m _____

Loch Ness

③

Highland Mountains

River Tay

Highland Games

Edinburgh

②

Seabird Centre

N

| river | mountain | lake | sea | ~~Highland Games~~ | castle |

2 💿 ✏️ **Listen and number.**

① on Monday ② on Tuesday ③ on Wednesday ④ on Thursday ⑤ on Friday

3 ✏️ **Fill in your portfolio.**

Sally 4 Activity Book Förderheft © 2015 Cornelsen Schulverlage GmbH, Berlin

Jobs

1  **Listen and draw lines.**

 ④ Susan

 ⑥ Phil

 ① Liz

 ② Eric

 ③ Tim

 ⑤ Emily

shop assistant

policewoman

_____

_____

_____

_____

2 ✎ **Write the correct jobs next to the pictures.**

~~shop assistant~~   ~~policewoman~~   teacher   doctor   hairdresser   millionaire

3 💬 🧒🧒 **Tell your partner: Liz** wants to be a **policewoman.** ...

Sally 4 Activity Book Förderheft © 2015 Cornelsen Schulverlage GmbH, Berlin

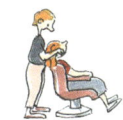

Jobs around the house

I have to …	Tick ✔: yes or no	Ask your group: Do you have to …? Count: How many say yes? (卌)
I have to make my bed.	☐ Yes, I do. ☐ No, I don't.	Do you have to make your bed?
… help in the garden.	☐ Yes, I do. ☐ No, I don't.	… help in the garden?
… do my homework.	☐ Yes, I do. ☐ No, I don't.	… do your homework?
… feed my pet.	☐ Yes, I do. ☐ No, I don't.	… feed your pet?
… help in the kitchen.	☐ Yes, I do. ☐ No, I don't.	… help in the kitchen?
… tidy my room.	☐ Yes, I do. ☐ No, I don't.	… tidy your room?
I have to _____	☐ Yes, I do. ☐ No, I don't.	Do you have to _____ ?

> walk the dog   babysit   do the shopping   lay the table

1 ✎ **What are your jobs?**

2 🦘 **Do a class survey. Ask and count.**

3 ✎ **Fill in your portfolio.**

Do you have to tidy your room?

I have to tidy my pouch!

Salty 4 Activity Book Förderheft © 2015 Cornelsen Schulverlage GmbH, Berlin

Dialogues

1 ✂️🖍️ Cut out the speech bubbles 💬 (page 45). Match and stick in.

2 ✏️ Write your own dialogue.

3 🐾 Write a dialogue with your partner. Act it out.

Where are you from?

What language do you speak?

It's three o'clock.

Where's the cat?

It's Wednesday.

Yes, I'd like a coke, please.

Sally 4 Activity Book Förderheft © 2015 Cornelsen Schulverlage GmbH, Berlin

Can you play the guitar?

Hello, how are you?

Yes, I'd like a new pullover, please.

It's 70 pence.

How can I go from here to Victoria Station?

What's the matter?

My hobby is playing football.

4 ✎ **Fill in your portfolio.**

Sally 4 Activity Book Förderheft © 2015 Cornelsen Schulverlage GmbH, Berlin

 Guy Fawkes

The story of Guy Fawkes

1 **Read the text.**

Long, long ago,  was king of England.

 **and his** **didn't like** . They had a terrible plan.

 : I hate . I want to kill him!  : Yes, let's kill !

 : Listen, my ! I've got a plan. **Let's blow up the** .

 : Yes, let's blow up the . We need lots of .

 and his  put 36 boxes of  in a room under

the . That was on the 5th of November 1604.

But the plan didn't work.

 and his  were put into prison in the .

The were happy that was safe and had

a big in the street.

 : Long live ! Long live !

Today, on the 5th of November, we still celebrate **Night**

with a big **and fireworks.**

Sally 4 Activity Book Förderheft © 2015 Cornelsen Schulverlage GmbH, Berlin

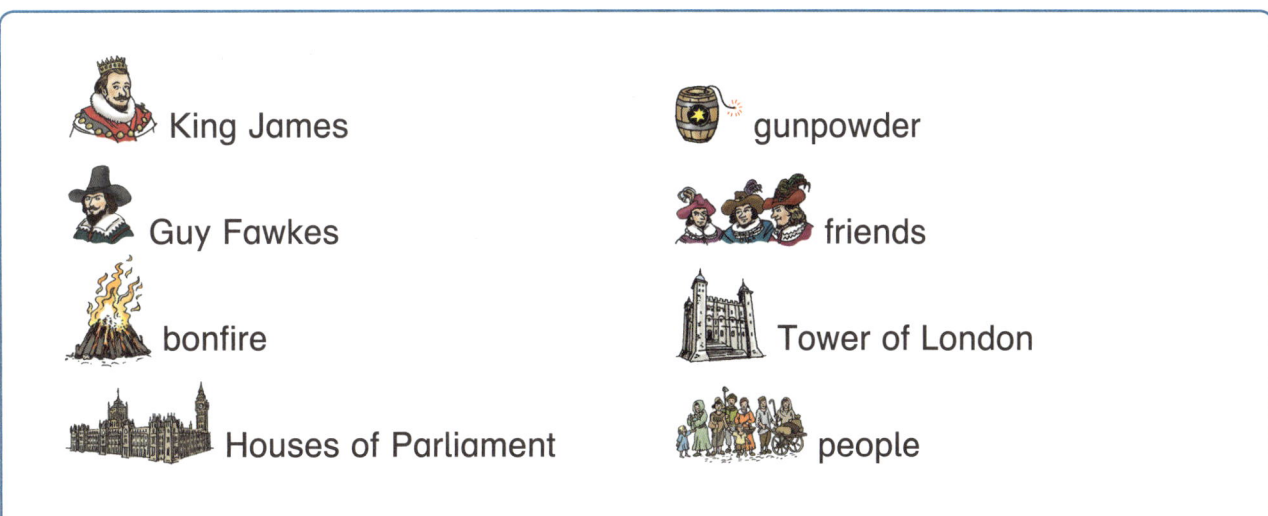

King James

gunpowder

Guy Fawkes

friends

bonfire

Tower of London

Houses of Parliament

people

2 ✎ **Read and tick ✔ the correct answers.**

Guy Fawkes Day is

☐ on 5th November.

☐ on 5th December.

☐ in summer.

Guy Fawkes wanted to blow up

☐ the Tower of London.

☐ the Houses of Parliament.

☐ Tower Bridge.

Guy Fawkes didn't like

☐ King George.

☐ King James.

☐ King John.

3 ✎ **Fill in your portfolio.**

I like bonfires!

Sally 4 Activity Book Förderheft © 2015 Cornelsen Schulverlage GmbH, Berlin

Let's be thankful!

1 ✎ **Listen and colour.**

2 ✎ **Count and write.**

5	_____
4	potatoes
7	_____
12	beans
2	corncobs

1	_____
3	_____
6	_____
8	_____

carrots   ~~potatoes~~   tomatoes   ~~beans~~   ~~corncobs~~
pumpkin   apples   plums   pears

3 ✎ **What are you thankful for? Write it down.**

I'm thankful for _____ .

my home   my family   my friends   my teacher   my toys   …

Sally 4 Activity Book Förderheft © 2015 Cornelsen Schulverlage GmbH, Berlin

Thanksgiving Day

1 ✏️ **How does Carol's family celebrate Thanksgiving Day?**
Read and tick ✔ the correct sentences.

☐ Mum gets up at 10 o'clock.

☐ She puts the cake into the oven.

☐ My family comes together for the Thanksgiving dinner.

☐ We have turkey, chips and hamburgers.

☐ We go to the Thanksgiving parade.

☐ In the evening we watch the tennis match on TV.

2 ✏️ **Write a little eleven.**

_____

_____ pie

turkey _____ _____

corncobs _____ _____ family

fun

3 **Read the comic.**

Hello, turkey! Come to my Thanksgiving dinner.

Oh no! Don't eat me!

You are my guest for Thanksgiving.

Sally 4 Activity Book Förderheft © 2015 Cornelsen Schulverlage GmbH, Berlin

A story about the first Thanksgiving

1  **Write the story in your own Indian signs.
Show it to your group.**

Little Bear

sees

a ship.

Little Bear

sees

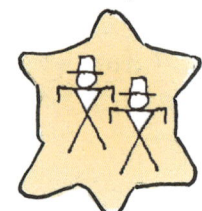

some white people.

The Indians help

the white people

to build their houses,

to plant corn,

to hunt turkeys

and to catch fish.

The Indians

and the white people

have a big party:

the first Thanksgiving.

⭐ **Find out and learn about the American Indians on the Internet.**

2 ✎ **Fill in your portfolio.**

Sally 4 Activity Book Förderheft © 2015 Cornelsen Schulverlage GmbH, Berlin

✂ Numbers (page 3)

✂ Through the day (page 16)

At eight o'clock in the morning I get up and eat. I have some milk and some cornflakes with sugar – so it's sweet.	**At three o'clock in the afternoon** school is over – hooray! I go home and watch TV, have fun with my friends and play.
At nine o'clock in the morning I'm already at school. I learn till I hear the bell ring for lunchtime and that's cool.	**At eight o'clock in the evening** I read and go to bed. Then I turn all the lights off and say: "Good night!" to Mum and Dad.

✂ In the shop (page 22)

It's too big.	Thank you.	Here you are.
Yes, please. I'd like a new jacket.	It's perfect. How much is it?	

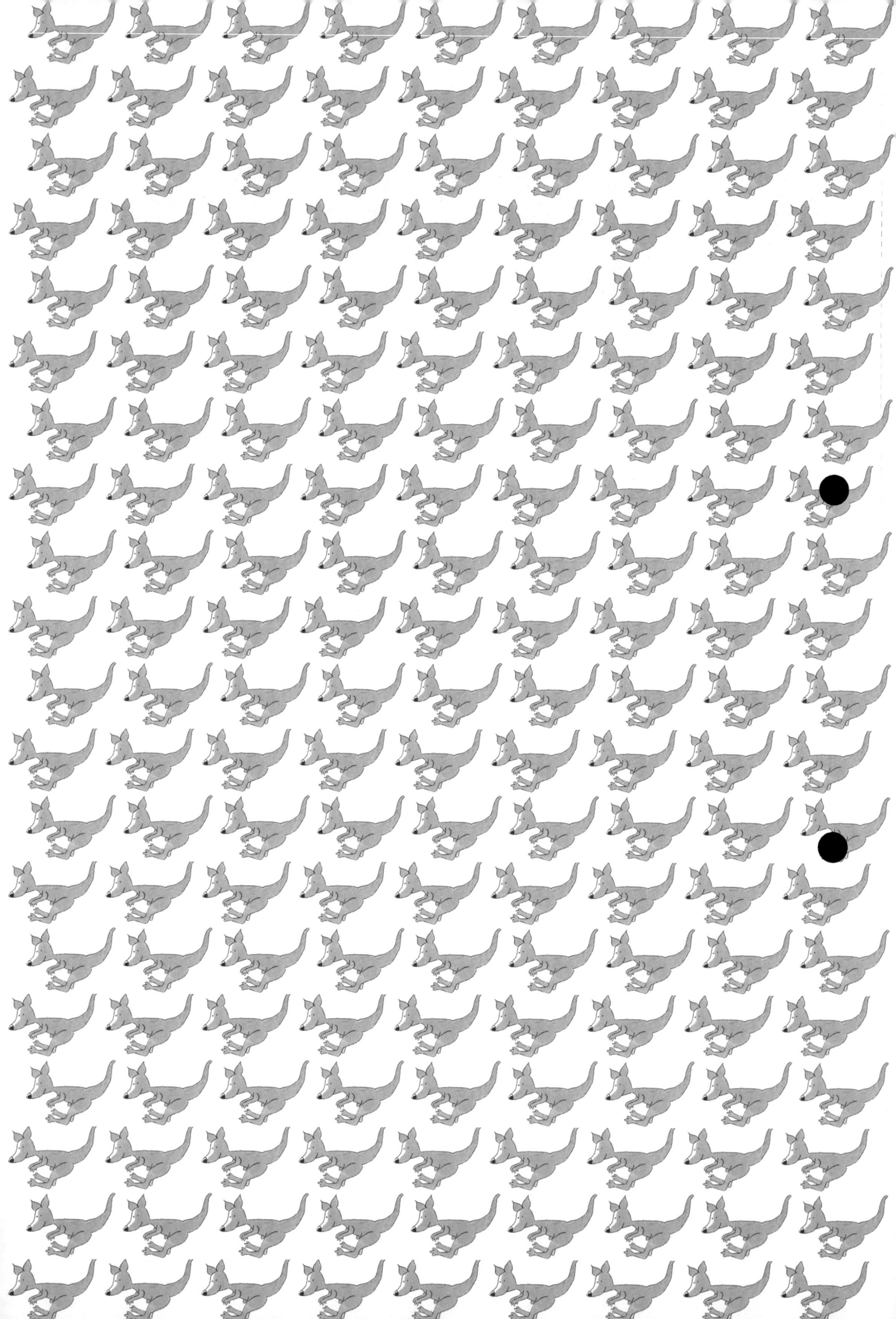

✂ One day in the life of Alpha 72 (page 17)

✂ The inline skating accident (page 31)

Ready, steady, go!	Next, please.	My leg hurts so much. And my hand hurts, too.
Your leg is broken.	Let's go to the doctor's.	

✂ Dialogues (pages 36, 37)

I'm from Australia.	It's under the sofa.
What day is it today?	I speak English.
What time is it?	Would you like something to drink?

Can I help you?	How much is it?	You can take the underground.
I'm fine, thank you.	My leg hurts.	
What's your hobby?	No, I can't.	

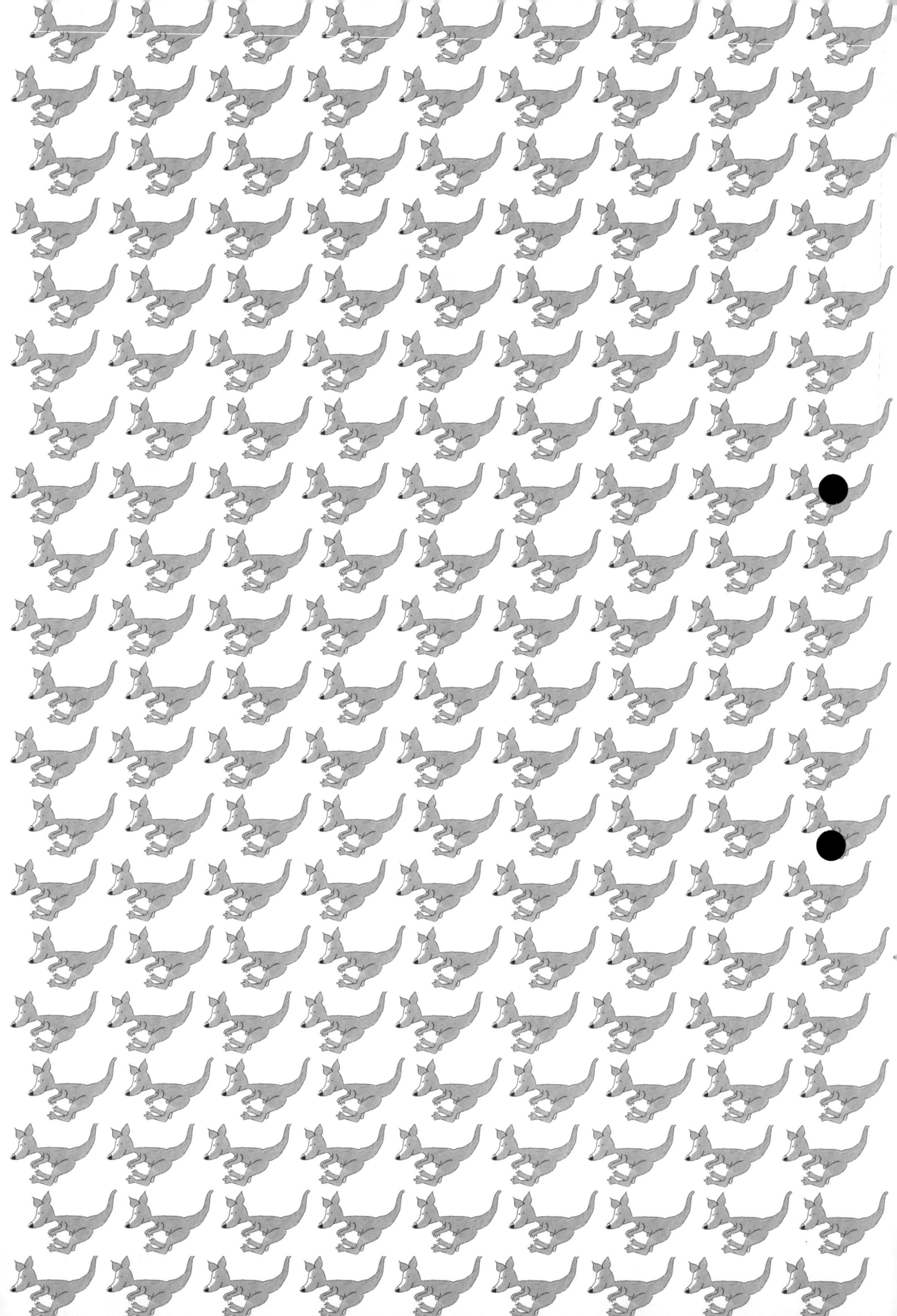

✂ Jack and the beanstalk (page 23)

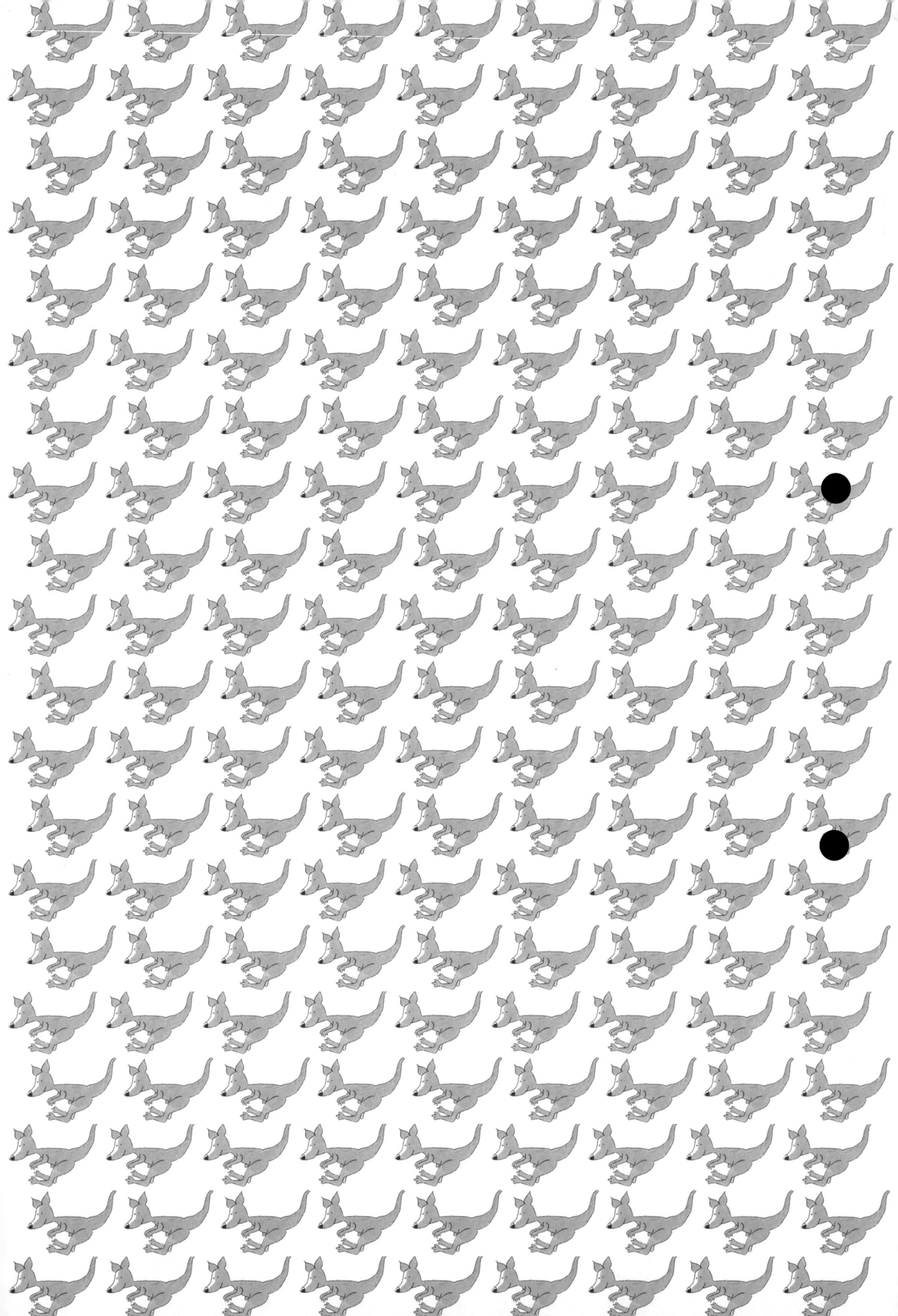

Mein Sprachenportfolio
Klasse 4

My name is _____ .

I'm in class _____ at _____ .

So habe ich
im Englischunterricht gearbeitet:

	1. Halbjahr	2. Halbjahr
Ich habe aufmerksam zugehört.	🟢🟡🔴	🟢🟡🔴
Ich habe mich regelmäßig gemeldet.	🟢🟡🔴	🟢🟡🔴
Ich habe versucht, neue Wörter genau nachzusprechen.	🟢🟡🔴	🟢🟡🔴
Ich habe versucht, in Gesprächen möglichst viel auf Englisch zu sagen.	🟢🟡🔴	🟢🟡🔴
Ich habe die Lieder mitgesungen.	🟢🟡🔴	🟢🟡🔴
Ich habe mindestens einen Reim gründlich geübt und aufgesagt.	🟢🟡🔴	🟢🟡🔴
Ich habe bei den Hörübungen genau zugehört.	🟢🟡🔴	🟢🟡🔴
Ich konnte verstehen, was meine Lehrerin / mein Lehrer auf Englisch sagt.	🟢🟡🔴	🟢🟡🔴
Ich habe Wörter richtig abgeschrieben.	🟢🟡🔴	🟢🟡🔴
Ich konnte schon kleine Texte schreiben.	🟢🟡🔴	🟢🟡🔴

Sally 4 Activity Book Förderheft © 2015 Cornelsen Schulverlage GmbH, Berlin

Diese Wörter kenne ich und kann ich aufschreiben:

_____   _____

_____   _____

_____   _____

_____   _____

_____   _____

_____   _____

cat	blue	butter	shoes	apple	tea	red
dog	bread	book	pen	T-shirt		

Weitere Wörter, die ich oft benutzt und mir gut gemerkt habe:

_____

_____

Das möchte ich im 4. Schuljahr lernen:

_____

_____

_____

1 ✏️ **Diese Zahlen kann ich benennen:** ✔

Hilfe findest du im Activity Book auf Seite 3.

10	30	40	80	90
☐	☐	☐	☐	☐

20	50	60	70	100
☐	☐	☐	☐	☐

2 ✏️ **Ich kann jemanden nach der Uhrzeit fragen:**

What _____ is it, please?

> time   It's   twelve   five

3 ✏️ **Ich kann sagen, wie spät es ist:**

 It's _____ o'clock.

 _____ half past _____.

4 **Das kann ich auch schon auf Englisch:**

Ich kann den Rap „Welcome back to school" mitsprechen.

Ich konnte viele Aufgaben des Spiels im Pupil's Book richtig lösen.

Ich kann das Lied „100 little kangaroos are sitting on Big Ben" singen.

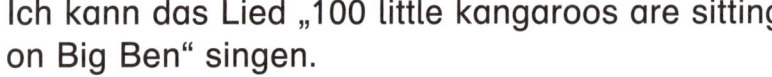

Sally 4 Activity Book Förderheft © 2015 Cornelsen Schulverlage GmbH, Berlin

1 ✎ **Diese Räume kann ich benennen:** ✔

Hilfe findest du im Activity Book auf Seite 6.

 ☐    ☐   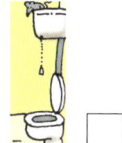 ☐

 ☐    ☐

2 ✎ **Ich kenne diese Möbelstücke:**

Male oder klebe sie auf. Schreibe das englische Wort dazu.

3 ✎ **Ich kann sagen, ob etwas zu groß, zu klein oder genau richtig ist:**

Hilfe findest du im Activity Book auf Seite 7 und im Pupil's Book auf Seite 8.

The chair is too _____

The bed is _____

The wardrobe is too _____

big   small
just right

4 **Das hat mir geholfen, die Geschichte „Gavin the ghost" zu verstehen:**

_____

_____

1 ✎ **Für mein Lieblingssandwich brauche ich:**

Hilfe findest du im Activity Book auf Seite 8 und im Pupil's Book auf Seite 9.

_____

_____

bread   tomato   ham   cheese   lettuce   ketchup

2 ✎ **Diese Gegenstände kann ich benennen und aufschreiben:**

Hilfe findest du im Activity Book auf Seite 10.

_____   _____

_____   _____

_____   _____

plate   cup   glass   knife   fork   spoon

3 **Das kann ich auch schon auf Englisch:**

Ich kenne verschiedene Mittagsgerichte.

Ich habe verstanden, was Phil und Emily bestellt haben.

Ich kann selbst etwas zum Essen oder Trinken bestellen.

Ich kann den „Sandwich Rap" mitsingen.

4 ✎ **So habe ich eine Strophe des „Sandwich Rap"
auswendig geübt:**

_____

_____

Sally 4 Activity Book Förderheft © 2015 Cornelsen Schulverlage GmbH, Berlin

1 ✎ **Diese Hobbys kann ich benennen und aufschreiben:**

Hilfe findest du im Activity Book auf Seite 12.

_____

riding a horse

_____

_____

_____

| playing football   reading books   swimming   ~~riding a horse~~ |

My hobby is _____.

2 Das kann ich auch schon auf Englisch:

Ich kann einen Steckbrief über mich und meine
Hobbys schreiben.

Ich habe das Interview mit Dirk Nowitzki gehört und verstanden.

Ich habe selbst ein Interview gemacht und als Rollenspiel
vorgeführt.

Ich kann den „Sporty Rap" mitsprechen.

3 Feedback

Das hat mir in dieser Unit am meisten Spaß gemacht:

_____

Das hat mir nicht gefallen:

_____

Sally 4 Activity Book Förderheft © 2015 Cornelsen Schulverlage GmbH, Berlin

1 ✎ **Ich kann sagen, was ich im Tagesverlauf mache:**

Hilfe findest du im Activity Book auf den Seiten 16 und 17 und
im Pupil's Book auf Seite 13.

Monday   Tuesday
Wednesday
Thursday   Friday

Today is _____ .

At _____ o'clock in the morning I _____ .

_____

At _____ o'clock in the afternoon I _____ .

At _____ o'clock in the evening I _____ .

go to bed   read a book   have lunch   go to school
go home   have breakfast   do my homework   watch TV

2 **Das kann ich auch schon auf Englisch:**

Ich kann die Geschichte „Emily's day" verstehen.   ○ ○ ○

Ich kann das Lied „Through the day" singen.   ○ ○ ○

Ich habe die Bilder zur Geschichte von Alpha 72
zugeordnet und die fehlenden Wörter eingetragen.   ○ ○ ○

Ich kann die Geschichte „At the same time" verstehen
und ein Minibuch dazu basteln.   ○ ○ ○

3 ✎ **Das ist mein Lieblingssatz aus „At the same time":**

Hilfe findest du im Pupil's Book auf Seite 14.

_____

_____

_____

Sally 4 Activity Book Förderheft © 2015 Cornelsen Schulverlage GmbH, Berlin

1 ✎ **Ich kann viele Dinge benennen und aufschreiben, die man im Supermarkt kaufen kann:**

Hilfe findest du im Activity Book auf Seite 18 und im Pupil's Book auf Seite 15.

apples   eggs   cheese   chocolate

2 **So bin ich mit schwierigen Wörtern beim Lesen der Geschichte „Something good" umgegangen:** ✔

☐ Ich habe Wörter im Wörterbuch nachgeschlagen.

☐ Ich konnte mir die Bedeutung einiger Wörter aus dem Zusammenhang der Geschichte selbst erklären.

☐ Ich habe mir Wörter deutlich vorsprechen lassen.

☐ Ich habe den Text mehrmals von der CD gehört.

☐ Ich habe meine/n Lehrer/in oder Mitschüler gefragt.

Sally 4 Activity Book Förderheft © 2015 Cornelsen Schulverlage GmbH, Berlin

3 ✎ **Ich kann die Geschäfte in einem Einkaufszentrum benennen:** ✓

Hilfe findest du im Activity Book auf den Seiten 20 und 21.

 ☐

 ☐

 ☐

 ☐

 ☐

 ☐

 ☐

 ☐

4 **Das kann ich auch schon auf Englisch:**

Ich kann verstehen, was Emily, Liz, Eric und Phil im Supermarkt einkaufen.

○ ○ ○

Ich kann sagen, auf welcher Etage des Einkaufszentrums ein Geschäft ist.

○ ○ ○

Ich kann den Hörtext von Liz und Phil im Kleidungsgeschäft verstehen.

○ ○ ○

Ich kann mit einem Partner ein Verkaufsgespräch vorspielen.

○ ○ ○

Sally 4 Activity Book Förderheft © 2015 Cornelsen Schulverlage GmbH, Berlin

1 ✎ **Diese Wörter kann ich benennen und aufschreiben:**

Hilfe findest du im Activity Book auf Seite 23 und im Pupil's Book auf Seite 18.

_____   _____   _____   _____

> beans   cow   pie   giant

2 ✎ **Ich kann die Sätze den Bildern zuordnen:**

1	We must sell the cow.
2	Jack climbs up the beanstalk.
3	Fee, fi, foe, fum, I smell the blood of an Englishman.

3 **So habe ich geübt, den Text zu lesen:** ✔

☐ Ich habe mir den Text vorsprechen lassen.

☐ Ich habe mir den Text selbst laut vorgelesen.

☐ Ich habe mit einem Partner lesen geübt.

4 **Feedback**

Das hat mir in dieser Unit am meisten Spaß gemacht:

_____

Das hat mir nicht gefallen:

_____

1  **Diese Wörter kann ich benennen und aufschreiben:**

Hilfe findest du im Pupil's Book auf Seite 20.

_____   _____   _____

_____   _____   _____

bus   ferry   plane   train   taxi   underground   skateboard   car

Ich kenne auch noch diese Fortbewegungsmittel:

_____   _____

2 **Ich kann die Geschichte „Detective Brighthead" verstehen.**

Diese Verkehrsmittel kommen in der Geschichte vor: ✔

☐    ☐    ☐

☐    ☐    ☐

3  **Das kann ich auch schon auf Englisch:**

Hilfe findest du im Activity Book auf Seite 26.

Ich kann fragen, wie ich zum London Eye komme:

_____

to the London Eye?   can I   How   get

Sally 4 Activity Book Förderheft © 2015 Cornelsen Schulverlage GmbH, Berlin

1 ✎ **Diese Tiere kann ich benennen und aufschreiben:**

Hilfe findest du im Activity Book auf Seite 27.

_____ _____ _____ _____

_____ _____ _____ _____

monkey   lion   zebra   snake   hippo   elephant   giraffe   tortoise

2 ✎ **Ich kann sagen und aufschreiben, wie die Tiere sind:**

Hilfe findest du im Activity Book auf den Seiten 27 und 29.

The hippo is _____ .

The giraffe is _____ .

The lion is _____ .

The monkey is _____ .

funny   tall   fat   dangerous

3 ✎ **Ich kann das Tier-Rätsel lösen:**

It's grey and very big.
It has got four legs and a trunk.
It lives in the jungle.
It eats leaves and grass.

It's an _____ .

4 ✎ **Ich kann selbst ein Tier-Rätsel aufschreiben:**

_____

_____

It's _____ .

Sally 4 Activity Book Förderheft © 2015 Cornelsen Schulverlage GmbH, Berlin

5 **Das hat mir geholfen, die Geschichte „The clever tortoise"
zu verstehen:** ✔

☐ Ich habe mir vorgestellt, was in der Geschichte passiert.

☐ Ich habe mir die Bilder im Pupil's Book angesehen.

☐ Ich habe den Text in den Sprechblasen mitgelesen.

☐ Ich habe beim Hören auf Wörter geachtet, die ich schon kenne.

6 **Das kann ich auch schon auf Englisch:**

Ich kann das Lied „Walking through the jungle" singen.   ○ ○ ○

Ich kann den Reim „Five little monkeys" mitsprechen.   ○ ○ ○

Ich kann mein Tier-Rätsel vortragen.   ○ ○ ○

7 **Feedback**

Das hat mir in dieser Unit am meisten Spaß gemacht:

_____

_____

Das hat mir nicht gefallen und das fand ich schwierig:

_____

_____

Sally 4 Activity Book Förderheft © 2015 Cornelsen Schulverlage GmbH, Berlin

1 ✎ **Diese Wörter kann ich benennen und aufschreiben:**

Hilfe findest du im Activity Book auf Seite 30.

> headache   earache
> backache   neckache

2 ✎ **Ich kann sagen, wenn mir etwas weh tut:**

Hilfe findest du im Activity Book auf Seite 30.

My _____ hurts.

> back   head   ear   neck

I've got a _____ .

3 ✎ **Ich weiß, was man bei bestimmten Verletzungen tun muss:**

Hilfe findest du im Pupil's Book auf Seite 29.

_____

_____

Diese Telefonnummer rufe ich im Notfall an: _____

4 **Das kann ich auch schon auf Englisch:**

Ich kann das Lied „The Hokey Cokey" mitsingen
und die Bewegungen dazu machen.

○ ○ ○

Ich kann den Comic „At the doctor's" verstehen und weiß,
warum alle Tiere aus dem Behandlungszimmer fliehen.

○ ○ ○

Ich kann die Geschichte „The inline skating accident" verstehen.

○ ○ ○

Sally 4 Activity Book Förderheft © 2015 Cornelsen Schulverlage GmbH, Berlin

1 ✎ **Diese Dinge kann ich benennen und aufschreiben:**

Hilfe findest du im Activity Book auf Seite 33 und im Pupil's Book auf Seite 31.

_____   _____   _____

Highland Games

_____   _____

river   lake   mountain   castle   Nessie   ~~Highland Games~~

2 **Das kann ich auch schon auf Englisch:**

Ich kann die Geschichte „Sally and the Loch Ness Monster"
verstehen.

Ich kann sagen, was sich die Familie Brown in Schottland
ansehen will.

3 ✎ **Das weiß ich jetzt über Schottland:**

Hier ist Platz für deine Ideen. Du kannst alles aufschreiben, was du weißt,
Bilder aus Prospekten einkleben und beschriften usw.

Sally 4 Activity Book Förderheft © 2015 Cornelsen Schulverlage GmbH, Berlin

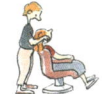

1 **Diese Berufe kann ich benennen und aufschreiben:**
Hilfe findest du im Activity Book auf Seite 34 und im Pupil's Book auf Seite 33.

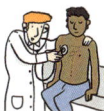      

_____ _____ _____

_____ _____ vet

policeman   doctor   teacher   hairdresser   ~~vet~~   shop assistant

2 **Das sind meine Eltern, Verwandte oder Bekannte von Beruf:**

My mother is a _____

My _____ is a _____

3 **Das kann ich auch schon auf Englisch:**
Hilfe findest du im Pupil's Book auf Seite 33.

Ich kann andere Kinder fragen, was sie werden wollen: ✔

☐ What do you want to be?

Ich kann sagen, was ich werden will:

☐ I want to be a _____.

4 **Diese Aufgaben erledige ich zu Hause:**
Hilfe findest du im Pupil's Book auf Seite 34 und im Activity Book auf Seite 35.

I have to _____

make my bed   do my homework   tidy my room

Sally 4 Activity Book Förderheft © 2015 Cornelsen Schulverlage GmbH, Berlin

1 ✎ **Diesen Flaggen kann ich eine Sprache zuordnen:**

Hilfe findest du im Pupil's Book auf Seite 36.

_____

_____

_____

_____

Spanish

_____

English   German   Turkish   ~~Spanish~~   Greek   Italian

2 **Das kann ich auch schon auf Englisch:**

Ich kann das Lied „We all live in the same world" singen.

Ich kann einen Freund oder eine Freundin beschreiben.

3 ✎ **Das hat mir geholfen, unbekannte Wörter in der Geschichte „A rainbow of friends" zu verstehen: ✔**

☐ Ich habe mir die Bilder im Pupil's Book angesehen.

☐ Ich habe mir das Wort aus dem Zusammenhang erschlossen.

☐ Ich kenne ein ähnlich klingendes Wort in einer anderen Sprache.

4 ✎ **Dieses Gespräch aus dem Activity Book (S. 36 und 37) habe ich mir besonders gut gemerkt: ✔**

☐ Hello, how are you? – I'm fine, thank you.

☐ What time is it? – It's three o'clock.

☐ _____

Sally 4 Activity Book Förderheft © 2015 Cornelsen Schulverlage GmbH, Berlin

1 ✎ **Diese Bilder aus der Geschichte zu Guy Fawkes kann ich benennen:** ✔

Hilfe findest du im Activity Book auf den Seiten 38 und 39 und im Pupil's Book auf Seite 37.

 ☐

 ☐

 ☐

 ☐

 ☐

2 **Das kann ich auch schon auf Englisch:**

Ich kann die Geschichte von Guy Fawkes lesen und verstehen. ○ ○ ○

Ich kann die Fragen zur Geschichte beantworten. ○ ○ ○

Ich kann das Lied „Bonfire Night" singen. ○ ○ ○

3 ✗ **Das weiß ich jetzt über Guy Fawkes:**

Hier ist Platz für deine Ideen. Du kannst alles aufschreiben, was du weißt, malen, Bilder aufkleben und beschriften usw.

1  **Diese Wörter kann ich benennen:** ✔

Hilfe findest du im Activity Book auf den Seiten 40 und 41 und im
Pupil's Book auf Seite 39.

 ☐

 ☐

 ☐

 ☐

 ☐

 ☐

2  **Das weiß ich jetzt über Thanksgiving und die USA:**

Hier ist Platz für deine Ideen. Du kannst alles aufschreiben, was du weißt,
malen, Bilder aufkleben und beschriften usw.

3 **Das kann ich auch schon auf Englisch:**

Ich kann die Geschichte von Carol's Thanksgiving verstehen.

Ich habe die „Story about the first Thanksgiving" verstanden
und eigene Schriftzeichen dazu erfunden.

Ich kann das Lied „Wichi Tei" singen.

Ich kann ein Thanksgiving-Elfchen schreiben.

Sally 4 Activity Book Förderheft © 2015 Cornelsen Schulverlage GmbH, Berlin

1 ✎ **Diese Wörter kann ich benennen:** ✔

Hilfe findest du im Pupil's Book auf den Seiten 41 und 42.

 ☐  ☐  ☐

 ☐  ☐  ☐

2 ✎ **Das weiß ich jetzt über Australien:**

Hier ist Platz für deine Ideen. Du kannst alles aufschreiben, was du weißt, malen, Bilder aufkleben und beschriften usw.

3 **Das kann ich auch schon auf Englisch:**

Ich kann die Geschichte „Father Christmas in Australia" verstehen. ⬡⬡⬡

Ich kann das Lied „The five days of Christmas" singen. ⬡⬡⬡

Ich habe den Text „Let's go to Australia" gehört und kann die Sätze lesen und verstehen. ⬡⬡⬡

1  **Diese Wörter kann ich benennen:** ✔

Hilfe findest du im Pupil's Book auf den Seiten 44 und 52.

  □  □  □

□

Ich kann auf Englisch „Frohe Ostern" wünschen:

_____

2 **Das hat mir beim Basteln der Osterkarte geholfen:** ✔

☐ Ich habe die Anleitung im Pupil's Book mehrmals gelesen.

☐ Ich habe mir die Bilder genau angesehen.

☐ Wir haben uns in der Gruppe geholfen.

3 **Das kann ich auch schon auf Englisch:**

Ich kann das Lied „I like the flowers" singen.

Ich kann noch ein anderes Osterlied singen
oder ein Gedicht aufsagen.

4  **Feedback**

Das hat mir in dieser Unit am meisten Spaß gemacht:

_____

Das hat mir nicht gefallen und das fand ich schwierig:

_____

Sally 4 Activity Book Förderheft © 2015 Cornelsen Schulverlage GmbH, Berlin

Hier sammle ich meine Lieblingswörter zu den verschiedenen Themen:

Time and numbers	At home
Lunch	Hobbies and sports
Shopping	Transport

Sally 4 Activity Book Förderheft © 2015 Cornelsen Schulverlage GmbH, Berlin

Hier sammle ich meine Lieblingswörter zu den verschiedenen Themen: Im letzten Feld kannst du eine eigene Überschrift wählen.

Animals	At the doctor's
Scotland	Jobs
Special days	_____

Sally 4 Activity Book Förderheft © 2015 Cornelsen Schulverlage GmbH, Berlin